YOUR KNOWLEDGE HAS VALUE

Margarita Apyestina

Does CLIL (content and language integrated learning) need its own methodology?

GRIN Verlag

Bibliografische Information der Deutschen Nationalbibliothek:

Die Deutsche Bibliothek verzeichnet diese Publikation in der Deutschen National-
bibliografie; detaillierte bibliografische Daten sind im Internet über http://dnb.d-
nb.de/ abrufbar.

Imprint:

Copyright © 2011 GRIN Verlag GmbH
Druck und Bindung: Books on Demand GmbH, Norderstedt Germany
ISBN: 978-3-656-51462-6

This book at GRIN:

http://www.grin.com/en/e-book/262752/does-clil-content-and-language-integrated-
learning-need-its-own-methodology

Johann Wolfgang Gothe Universität Frankfurt / Main
Fachbereich 10: Neuere Philologien
Institut für England- und Amerikastudien WS 10/11
Seminar: CLIL- Content and Language Integrated Learning
Leistungsnachweis: "Kleine Hausarbeit"
Margarita Apyestina
08.03.2011

Does CLIL need its own methodology?

The concept of bilingual instruction in Germany has started with school subjects in French in

1963 as a result of the "Elysée- Vertrag": France and Germany wanted to realize their political

agreement of peace and friendship through cultural approximation on the societal level which

became known as the Franco-German Friendship Treaty, and as a result, schools such as the

"deutsch-französische Gymnasien" or "Lycées franco-allemands" were established in both

countries.

By 1987, the number of these schools had increased to 25. It is important to underline the fact that the
beginning of bilingual instruction in Germany is very closely related to the use of French, rather than
English, as a classroom language (Wolff 2007).

The reason for using especially English for content and language integrated learning (CLIL)

nowadays is its function as the global "lingua franca" which means that English is used in

such areas as traveling, business, economy, science and entertainment by both native and

non-native speakers of English to enable communication with speakers of different languages.

Germany holds more than 800 schools that offer CLIL in different modern languages,

especially English, whereas North Rhine-Westphalia is the German leader in the field of

CLIL: in the year 2006, it had 162 English CLIL schools, 23 schools with French CLIL and

15 schools with other languages such as Italian, Modern Greek, Russian, Spanish and Dutch

(Wolff 2007).

Since CLIL is special because it means teaching a content subject through a foreign

language, one expects to find a curriculum specially designed for CLIL but surprisingly it is

not the case as illustrated by Dieter Wolff: "Beyond the usual formal instructions, only a few

of the Länder have ministerial instructions setting out a curriculum." In this case, North

Rhine-Westphalia leads again since it has developed so called "recommendations" that are

similar to curricula in their structure and that concern most content subjects taught in the foreign language. Additionally, „[a]ll of the recommendations have a comprehensive appendix containing teaching aids for the specialist language used in the subjects, examples of sequences of lessons, and other materials" (Wolff 2007). Besides that, the German curriculum for the content subject is the basis for the bilingual recommendation. The development of the students' ability to use and correctly understand specialist terminology in both languages is emphasized since "[t]he discrepancy between the cognitive and the linguistic abilities of the learner is deemed the central problem in bilingual teaching of specialised subjects" (Wolff 2007). This discrepancy indicates that students may be able to know about a phenomenon cognitively but may not know the word for it either in their mother tongue or in the target language, or they might know the word for a phenomenon linguistically in both languages but might not know what concept hides behind the word cognitively.

Additionally, the recommendations contain the demand that not only subject specific knowledge should be provided in CLIL classes but "it must also include the sort of more general skills needed in all subjects. These include the use of images, graphs and tables" whose specialist terminology should be learned in foreign language classes according to Dieter Wolff (Wolff 2007). Another emphasis lies on textual work and on the ability to read and write about the subject in the foreign language.

Another important feature of CLIL is its advancement of intercultural lerning that needs a structural development since it constitutes a chance to change one's point of view on a topic, to see one's own country or even oneself from the perspective of other countries and to look at other nations from their own perspective. Therefore, a special competence is developed through CLIL that is known as the intercultural communicative competence or as the intercultural mediation competence "since content material is culturally coded, such as primary sources in the subject of history" (Müller-Hartmann / Schocker von Ditfurth 2004: 153). The authors Müller-Hartmann and Schocker von Ditfurth (2004: 154) also argue that CLIL develops cultural awareness and language awareness since it confronts learners with situations where learning strategies and study skills need to be applied. To understand this example more precise, the authors give the example of Mandela's autobiography that is easy to read but that also demands readings of complex texts on „Britsh imperialism in South Africa" (Müller-Hartmann / Schocker von Ditfurth ib.).

Another important aspect of CLIL that distinguishes it from foreign language classes was mentioned at the International CLIL Conference 2011 in Frankfurt/Main during a lecture: the materials and topics are authentic and thus the students can benefit from authentic communication. In contrast, foreign language classes and books work with fictious topics and re-enactments of daily life communication that does not allow students to speek freely but forces them to produce formulaic utterances. This type of learning is important at the beginning of L2 and must not to be rejected ,but to develop further competences it must be transgressed. Additionally, Wolff argues that CLIL provides a deeper processing of and a higher involvement in the target language since the material is authentic and does not need to be constructed artificially which is the case in foreign language classes (Wolff 1997).

Therefore, this paper advances the view that all kinds of German schools – this means comprehensive schools, "Förder-", "Haupt-" and "Realschulen" as well as "Gymnasien" – should get the possibility to benefit from the advantages of CLIL classes since not only an elite of "Gymnasium"-students will be confronted with a globalized world after finishing school where good subject knowledge and multilingualism determine one's future and one's quality of life. The purpose of CLIL is to prepare the students to orientate in a changing world, so why not prepare as many students as possible, students from all social and educational areas of life, and not only a handful who were lucky enough to attend a school that offered CLIL. Therefore, this paper argues that CLIL definitely needs its own methodology to access and integrate students in different situations and to help them cope with the "double burden" of a content subject and a foreign language.

Nevertheless, there are different perspectives on the need of a special methodology for CLIL such as represented by Nando Mäsch who has been a supporter of French CLIL in Germany for years. He argues that CLIL will succeed when the same methods are applied that account for good education in general. He presents a scheme of methods that range from teacher-centered teaching to learner-centered teaching and only if one keeps the balance between teacher- and learner-centered methods, the lessons will succeed either in CLIL or any other subject. He consideres such methods as "Lehrervortrag", "Fragend-reproduzierendes Verhalten" and "Fragend-entwickelndes Verhalten" as teacher-centered regarding the first method as the maximum of teacher-centering, whereas methods such as "Schülervortrag", "Gruppenarbeit" and "Partnerarbeit" are considered learner-centered considering "Schülervortrag" to be the most learner-centered method. Nervertheless, this does not always have to be the case that a lecture given by a student is more learner-centered that other methods as Thürmann points out (Thürmann 2010: 73). Finally, the concept of this so called balanced "Methodenwaage" is no special method for teaching CLIL and it might run the risk of bilingual "laissez-faire" instead of supporting education.

Another reasoning is that immersion is the right method for teaching CLIL which is represented by Henning Wode. Nevertheless, it remains unclear what the exact definition of immersion really is since some authors consider immersion to be "bathing" in the target language while others consider immersion to take place when more than 50% of the duration of the lesson are not the mother tongue (Zydatiß 2000: 26). Wode argues that immersion works well if the lessons are learner-centered which remains unevidenced and, additionally, cannot be regarded as a seroius methoddological approach (Thürmann 2010: 73).

Finally, the last position argues that, on the one hand, immersion is a quite effective method to teach a foreign language, but on the other hand, it is not useful in heterogeneous classes since not every student is exposed to the target language to the same extent outside the classes and therefore, the level of proficiency would not remain homogeneous. Therefore, Thürmann calls for a special methodology for CLIL since CLIL has made its way into the educational mainstream and is not reserved for or restricted to an educational elite anymore (Thürmann 2010: 75).

Consequently, after the acknowledgment that CLIL needs a fundament of its own methodology to be successful, basic approaches and methods of CLIL will be illustrated that constitute the starting point to develop concept and methoddologies for CLIL lessons. One indispensable component and at the same time the initial point of learning is *reception of language* since it constitutes the fundamental tool in any language acquisition. Therefore, Krashen's (1982) axiom of "linguistic input (slightly) above the learner's level of competence" serves CLIL very well since it is not always possible to find texts or other materials such as original sources and films at learners' level of proficiency. To make sure that the sutdents follow the lesson Rousseau recommends teachers to use repetitions and synonyms as well as to rephrase and to circumscribe one's utterances in order to give "the students many chances to understand the language" since there might be a risk that the students capitulate or feel overcharged by language input that is above their level of proficiency (Rousseau 1995: 123). Another useful kind of input are visual aids such as pictures and cartoons that encourage speaking and provide authentic topics of conversation. This point of reception can be summerized as "comprehensible input" as Thürmann puts it which is related or rather opposed to what Thürmann calles "comprehensible output" which means that learners do not produce native-like speech although being immersed into the target language environment (2010: 79). This was found out by Cummins and Swain (1986) who assume that "[t]here appears to be little social or cognitive pressure to produce language that reflects more appropriately or precisely their intended meaning" which is to analyze the correcntess of grammar since the peers and the teacher grasp the message anyway, therefore, the learners are not confronted with "negative input" which means critique and thus cannot improve (Cummins / Swain

1986).

Additionally, there is an emphasis on reading skills, especially on two kinds of reading in comrehensible input: developmental reading and functional reading whereas the first means "learning to read" and the second "reading to learn", and as Mohan states "[i]n developmental reading, the reading materials [...] are selected to teach basic reading skills, and the language and information is limited" whereas "[f]unctional reading materials are essentially the content textbooks themselves, and the aim is to help the students understand the concepts in them" (Mohan 1986: 14). Thürmann argues that developmental reading is taught in the foreign language classroom whereas functional reading is practiced in content subjects, therefore, CLIL teachers must guarentee the development of strategies to gain access to texts during functional reading. An example for such strategies are "Erschließungsstrategien" which means to derive unknown words from the context or from other languages to understand the concept in a text (Thürmann 2010: 81).

Another component of successful learning is *production.* Since speech production in CLIL classes takes place without pressure, the output is often affected by insufficiency in regard to native speakers' norms (as illustrated above). Therefore, CLIL teachers must be able to "brigde" between the learners' output and their intended message. "Bridging" can be done through paraphrasing the incorrect speech or through directing the speaker towards the correct forms through questions and hints (Thürmann ib.). Another important method is "code-switching" that is accompanied by disagreement between CLIL teachers since some of them want to teach monoligually while others allow code-switching. Code-switching is defined precisely by de Courcy as the "insertion of words from one language into speech or writing in another language [...]. Code-switiching may be conscious or unconscious" (de Courcy 1995: 91). Code-switching is as important as bringing since it was argued by Butzkamm (1997: 41) that the students want to know some central expressions to continue with the discussion which indicates interest and involvement into the subject, and that there are no reasons why the avoidance of the mother tongue should lead to any benefit. There was also emphasis on sepecial or technical terms that should be provided in CLIL classes so that the students could use it in their speech production. For example the "Kulsutministerium" of North Rhine-Westphalia had clear suggestions which technical terms should be used in CLIL classes. But nowadays there is an emphasis on the approach that the students' general terms that are close to the specialist terminology will transform into technical terms of the content subject along with the learning progression. According to Krechel (1996: 23f.) it should not be the aim of CLIL to drum as many technical terms as possible into the learners' speech or mind.

5

On the other hand, it is useful to provide phrases for classroom discourse to reduce the lack between the students' output and their intended message. This approach consists of two basic principles: first, of the basic learning and communication strategies and second, of the subject specific skills. Examples of these linguistic devices for the subject physics are: definition, classification, making inductions, stating laws, describing states and processes, working with graphs, diagrams, tables etc, basic mathematics, interpreting, writing reports. These linguistic devices are called functional categories or "funktionale Kategorien" that make a connection between the target language and the content subject. The students have to use the target language according to these functional categories to be able to work with the topics and concepts of the content subject. These functional categories of speech also exist for other subject such as social studies and science: identify, classify or define, describe, explain, conclude or argue, evaluate (Thürmann 2010: 84). They connect the target language use and the content subject by giving language a functional role of illustrating the concepts of the subject which means that language is authentically used and not only practiced.

The third component or rather a competence to be aspired in CLIL is *autonomy* which is defined by Little (1991: 4) as the

capacity – for detachment, critical reflection, decision-making, and independent action. It presupposes, but also entails, that the learner will develop a particular kind of psychological relation to the process and content of learning.

Thürmann argues that autonomous learners who are able to observe, analyze, reflect and decide independently and maturely have to be shaped or modelled. This shaping or modelling takes place when the learners assume three different roles in CLIL lessons during which they acquire different competences and study skills: firstly, there is the role of the "communicator" who uses language "in authentic communicative situations which results in "language learning competence", secondly, there is the "explorer/experimenter/analyst" who uses language in "experimentation with and analysis of foreign language" which leads to "language and cultural awareness", and finally, there is the learner as a "learner" who uses language "in observation and evaluation of learning processes" which again results in language learning competence. Thürmann argues that study skills and autonomy are developed best in a CLIL classroom (compared to foreign language classes) since the learners must use metacognitive skills – i.e. thinking about thinking and learning processes, for example during reading a content text and making plans how to get the concept out of it – since a conscious engagement in one's learning/understanding process takes place (Thürmann 2010: 85).

As for the conclusion of the theoretical methodology for CLIL, one can assume that the main focus lies on the development of what Jim Cummins called the cognitive/academic langauge proficiency (CALP), as well as on learner autonomy in such areas as autonomous learning and conscious use of learning strategies. All in all, CLIL aims to develop the learners' responsibility for their own learning and to guarantee an authentic foreign language use. This standards, again, go hand in hand with the challanges of the 21st century such as globalization, constant changes in social and political structures and the norm of speaking at least two foreign languages fluently.

Additionally, there exists a practically applied methodology for CLIL that was developed from approaches from Rhineland-Palatinate: The Bilingual Triangle pictured by Wolfgang Hallet (1998).

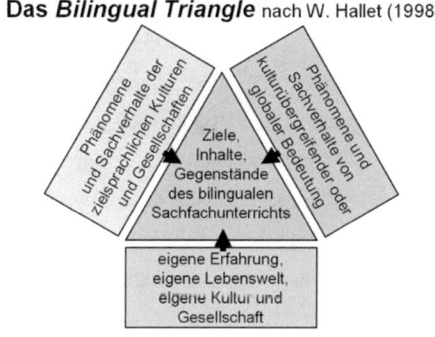

Das *Bilingual Triangle* nach W. Hallet (1998)

It consists of three main "Zielfelder" or target fields in which the students become proficient through CLIL. The first field is the ability to communicate about their own experiences, their living environment and their cultural environment: "own country and culture". This information is taught to them in geography, history, arts and social studies classes. The second field is the ability to communicate about the phenomena, the facts and issues of the target language country ("other countries and cultures"), whereas the third field is to become versed in cross-cultural, global or universal phenomena ("intercommunity") and to be well prepared for a communicative exchange in these areas (Hallet 1998: 119).

As Hallet points out, the bilingual content subjects are not congruent with the content subjects in the mother tongue in matters of topics and contents since CLIL integrates cross-culutural phenomena through the first target field of one's own culture. To integrate international issues into a content subject taught in the mother tongue would mean to reduce the time spent on the issues of one's own country. But in the context of CLIL the integration of the target field "other countries and cultures" means a cross-cultural gain (Hallet 1998: 120).

To illustrate the concept of the Bilingual Triangle, the design of a history unit will be given in the following. The unit "Wirtschaft und Gesellschaft in der mittelalterlichen Stadt. Medienvielfalt im bilingualen Geschichtsunterricht" was held in the school year 1995/96 in an 11th grade in a Gymnasium and was documented in a pedagogical paper. The unit was devided in five topics: 1. "Town and Town Dwellers: London around 1400", 2. "Guild", 3. "Frauen und Gewerbe in der mittelalterlichen Stadt", 4. "Medieval Merchants", 5. "The German Hanse". Hallet explains that although the second target field seems to dominate, the first target field was very well integrated into the lessons as well. For exaple the first topic "Town and Town Dwellers: London around 1400" was complemented by sources and questions concerning the students' home town Trier and an additional map of Trier was consulted to compare medieval Trier and to medieval London, and thus the two first target fields were combined (Hallet 1998: 123), whereas the 5th topic "The German Hanse" was based only on the first target field "own country and culture" (Hallet 1998: 123).

As for the third target field "intercommunity" Hallet suggests an improvement since it appeared only as a side-effect. He assumes that the third topic "Frauen und Gewerbe in der mittelalterlichen Stadt" would have been applicable to cover cross-cultural matters since it overlaps with other countries on a global level and its topical relevance to today's issues of gender equality is given. Additionally, the students showed great interest in the discussion of gernder equality, especially female students (Hallet ib.). This history unit design shows that all three target fields can be applied to a content subject without receiving a reduction in general knowledge of one's own country.

This paper concludes that CLIL works well for all kinds of schools if it is supported by an adequate methodology. Therefore, the methodology should be based upon the aim of the development of three main competences, namely reception, production and autonomy and should contain the three target fields as shown through the Bilingual Triangle. It is beyond all questions that all kinds of schools – including Hauptschulen and Förderschulen – are able to profit from CLIL and are capable of applying such methods as the Bilindual Triangle.

Butzkamm, Wolfgang (1997): „Zum Sprachwechsel im bilingualen Sachunterricht." In: Vollmer, Helmut J. / Thürmann, Eike (Hrsg.): Englisch als Arbeitssprache im Fachunterricht: Begegnung zwischen Theorie und Praxis. Gemeinsame Fachtagung der Deutschen Gesellschaft für Fremdsprachenforschung und des Landesinstituts für Schule und Weiterbildung, 30.01.-01.02.1997. Soest: 35-43.

Courcy, Michèle de (1995): 'You just live in French'. Adolescent learners' experiences of French immersion. In: Berthold, Michael (Hrsg.): Rising to the Bilingual Challenge. Canberra: The National Languages and Literacy Institute of Australia: 75-95.

Cummins, Jim / Swain, Merrill (1986): Bilingualism in Education. London and New York.

Hallet, Wolfgang (1998): Bilingual Tiangle, Überlegungen zu einer Didaktik des bilingualen Sachfachunterrichtes, in: Praxis des neusprachlichen Unterrichtes, Bd. 45: 117-125.

Krashen, Stephen D. (1982): Principles and Practice in Second Language Acquisition. Oxford.

Krechel, Hans-Ludwig (1996): Französisch als Vehikularsprache im bilingualen Sachfach Erdkunde. In: Buchloh, Paul-Gerhard et. al. (Hrsg.): Konvergenzen. Fremdprachenunterricht: Planung – Praxis – Theorie. Festschrift für Ingeborg Christ aus Anlaß ihres 60. Geburtstages. Tübingen: 17-33.

Little, David (1991): Learner Autonomy. 1: Definitions, Issues and Problems. Dublin.

Mohan, Bernard A. (1986): Language and Content: Reading, Mass.: Addison-Wesley.

Müller-Hartmann, Andreas / Schocker von Ditfurth, Marita (2004): Introduction to English Language Teaching. Stuttgart.

Rousseau, Emmanuelle (1995): Teaching sience through a second language. In: Berthold, Michael (Hrsg.): Rising to the Bilingual Challenge. Canberra: The National Languages and Literacy Institute of Australia: 121-149.

Thürmann, Eike (2010): Eine eigenständige Methodik für den bilingualen Sachfachunterricht? In: Bach, Gerd; Niemeier, S. (Hrsg.): Bilingualer Unterricht. Frankfurt / Main. S. 71-89.

Wolff, Dieter (1997): „Bilingualer Sachfachunterricht: Versuch einer lernpsychologischen und fachdidaktischen Begründung." In: Vollmer, Helmut J. / Thürmann, Eike (Hrsg.): Englisch als Arbeitssprache im Fachunterricht: Begegnung zwischen Theorie und Praxis. Gemeinsame Fachtagung der Deutschen Gesellschaft für Fremdsprachenforschung und des Landesinstituts für Schule und Weiterbildung, 30.01.-01.02.1997. Soest: 50-62.

Wolff, Dieter (2007): The History and Current Situation of Bilingual Instruction in Germany. Online im Internet: WWW: http://www.goethe.de/ges/spa/dos/ifs/met/de2747826.htm (01.03.2011)

Zydatiß, Wolfgang (2000): Bilingualer Unterricht in der Grundschule: Entwurf eines Spracherwerbskonzepts für zweisprachige Immersionsprogramme. Ismaning.